Flickering Shadows And Unseen Exits

Poems of Lost Light and Silent Streets

Arun Chandra

Dedication

To every unknown soul who drifted through my dusk,
whose quiet kindness bloomed like wildflowers
in the cracked pavement of my days
you, the fleeting shadows with hands outstretched,
who offered a glance when the stars turned cold,
a whisper of presence when silence grew heavy.
To the strangers whose footsteps brushed mine
on streets too loud to hear my name,
who paused beneath the flicker of a dying lamp
and saw me - not the ghost, not the echo,
but the trembling pulse beneath the weight.
Your kindness was a thread, thin as breath,
sewn into the fabric of my unraveling night.

To those who shared a bench, a breath, a burden
unasked, unthanked, unknown by daylight
you who carried your own unseen wounds
yet spared a shard of warmth for mine.
This book is yours, a lantern lit in return,
its glow a hymn to the grace you left behind,
to the souls who touched me softly
and vanished into the city's endless hum.
For you, who never knew your own light,
who walked away before the words could form

these verses rise like smoke from forgotten flames,
a tribute to the kindness that lingers,
unseen, unfading, in the corners of my being.

Preface

In the quiet spaces between breaths, where light trembles and shadows stretch, this book was born. It is not a map to escape, nor a guide to belonging, but a mirror held up to the moments when we feel most lost - within ourselves, within the clamor of a world that moves too fast to notice. These pages are the echoes of a mind pacing its own walls and a soul wandering streets that never lead home. They are the flicker of a candle lit in hope, only to reveal more darkness; the hum of a city that promises connection, only to drown it in noise.

Here, doors are myths we tell ourselves to keep going, and loneliness is a companion that knows us too well. The poems in Flickering Shadows and Unseen Exits do not offer answers - they ask questions that linger like smoke, curling around the edges of what we think we know. They are born from the tension between longing and fear, between the silence we carry and the silence we meet. Chapter 1, I Can't Find the Door, traces the contours of an inner prison, where every flame casts a shadow and every exit feels like an illusion. Chapter 2, Lonely Souls in a Busy City, steps into the pulse of urban life, where neon lights blind and crowds deafen, yet leave us unseen.

This is not a journey with a destination. It is a collection of moments—of staring at stars that no longer guide, of sitting still while the world blurs, of reaching for something that might not be there. If you find yourself in these words, it's not because I've found you, but because we've both been lost in the same flickering light. These poems are for the ones who feel the weight of their own thoughts, who walk among thousands and still hear only their own footsteps. They are for the seekers, the sitters, the silent - who know that sometimes the hardest doors to find are the ones we've locked ourselves.

Acknowledgements

No flame burns alone, not even the flickering ones that cast these shadows. This book, born from the quiet and the clamor, owes its breath to those who stood beside me - seen and unseen - through the nights when words were all I had.

To the voices that whispered encouragement when the silence grew too thick, you were the creak of a door I couldn't find, the echo that kept me searching. Your belief in these lines lit candles I didn't know I carried, and for that, I am endlessly grateful.

To the hands that held me steady when the walls closed in - friends, muses, keepers of my restless thoughts—you turned my pacing into poetry. You saw the cracks I couldn't, and in your presence, I learned to trace them without fear.

To the city itself, relentless and raw, you were both mirror and maze. Your streets taught me loneliness, but also the strange beauty of its shape. These pages are as much yours as mine, etched with the hum of your trains and the flicker of your lights.

To the poets and dreamers whose words came before, your verses were stars I followed when mine dimmed.

You showed me that even in the dark, there is a rhythm
worth writing, a truth worth chasing.
And to those who read these poems, who sit with them
as I once sat with my shadows - thank you. Your eyes
give these words a home, a place to rest after wandering.
If they resonate, it's because we've shared the same
unseen exits, the same lost light.

This is not a solitary work, though it sings of solitude. It
is a tapestry woven from countless threads - your
patience, your kindness, your quiet strength. To all of
you, named and unnamed, who helped me build this
fragile thing: my deepest thanks.

1. Whispers of a Hidden Exit

I sit, knees hugged tight in the cold corner of my bed
The night outside breathes heavily against the
windowpane
Stars blink like distant hopes, unreachable, indifferent
They no longer answer my silent wishes
Their shine dimmed by the storm I carry within
I lit a candle, thinking maybe fire can guide me
But it roared too loud, consuming the silence
Its heat blinded instead of lighting
The door I seek—if it even exists—remains a rumor
A myth told in my lonelier moments
And I'm still here, unmoving
Where escape feels like an illusion
And the prison is made of thought

2. Echoes of a Self-Made Cell

I've sat in the dark so long it feels like home
The walls breathe with my pain
Memories gather like dust in corners
And I wonder if I built this room myself
Each decision another brick
Each silence another nail
I thought I saw a handle once,
But when I reached, it vanished
Maybe the door isn't real
Maybe the only escape is surrender
To accept the night and stop searching

3. Jagged Stars and Lost Paths

Outside, they say the stars bring peace
But mine have sharp edges
They pierce instead of comfort
I lit a candle hoping to find clarity
But it exploded into chaos
Sparks in the silence
Now smoke clouds everything
And all I know is that I can't find the way
I stumble in thoughts that twist and turn
Each one leads me deeper
Further from the light I crave
The door remains missing
Or maybe I am

4. Jagged Stars and Lost PathsNew Poem

Outside, they say the stars bring peace
But mine have sharp edges
They pierce instead of comfort
I lit a candle hoping to find clarity
But it exploded into chaos
Sparks in the silence
Now smoke clouds everything
And all I know is that I can't find the way
I stumble in thoughts that twist and turn
Each one leads me deeper
Further from the light I crave
The door remains missing
Or maybe I am

5. Fading Maps and Silent Creaks

The stars used to be maps
But now they are mocking eyes
I try to read the sky for signs
But nothing answers back
I hold a flame close to my chest
But it offers no guidance
Only more shadows dancing on the wall
The door—I think I heard it once
A creak or a click, maybe
But I blinked and it disappeared
And now I'm left with echoes
And the burning question:
Is there even anything beyond this?

6. Screams of Light and Vanished Hopes

They told me light reveals the truth
So I struck a match
But all I saw was how empty everything really is
The flame roared like a scream
Too loud for answers
Too bright for comfort
The door vanished in that burst
Or maybe it never existed
Maybe I am searching for something
That doesn't want to be found

7. Whispers of Shadows and Fading Cracks

I have grown familiar with shadows
Their silence, their shape
They tuck me in at night
And whisper, "Stay"
The candle flares again
And for a second, I think I see it
A crack in the wall, a shimmer
But then it's gone
And all that remains
Is this room I cannot leave
Not because it's locked
But because I'm afraid
Of what might lie beyond

8. Flickering Faith and Silent Walls

The door is somewhere
I know it
I can feel it in the tremble of my breath
In the restless rhythm of my hands
I lit a candle, and another, and another
Until the room is full of flickering prayers
Still, the walls close in
Still, I cannot leave
The light only shows more darkness
The way forward blurs
I press my ear to every surface
Listening
But nothing calls me through

9. Cracks of Awareness and Treacherous Flames

There was a time I didn't need a door
Because I didn't realize I was inside something
Now, I know
Now, I claw at walls
Desperate for passage
I trace each crack like a map
Each silence like a possibility
But the flames betray me
They promise hope
And deliver more night
I am both prisoner and jailer
Longing for release
Terrified of what it means

Trembling Flames and Inner Doors. Trembling Flames and Inner Doors

Sometimes I think the door is within me
Hidden beneath layers of old pain
Buried under memories I refuse to unearth
I light a candle not to find the way
But to remember who I was
Before the world dimmed
Before silence swallowed sound
The flame trembles as I do
And maybe that's the key
Not to escape this place
But to ignite a path inward
Until the light grows strong enough
To make a door where none existed

11. Neon Pulse and Unseen Eyes

The city pulses with neon veins
People pour from subways like thoughts escaping a mind
Each face holds its own secret tragedy
But no one stops long enough to see
I wandered beneath flickering lamps
Looking for eyes that might meet mine
Just a glance, a pause, anything to say
I see you, you exist
But they walk past like shadows
Their headphones loud, their hearts louder
Everyone drowning in their own silence
And I sit on a weathered bench
Staring at the crowd like one stares at a flame
Drawn to it, burned by it
Alone, even in the center of everything

12. Echoes Overlooked in a Rushing Storm

At rush hour, I stand still while the world blurs
Footsteps slam into pavement like gunshots
Heels echo off glass walls
Laughter spills from restaurants with no memory of me
I try to speak
But my voice gets lost in the noise
So I wander
Not really heading anywhere
Hoping someone might notice
That I am not a building or a tree
That I am here
That I, too, am beating
But the city keeps its eyes forward
And I disappear

13. Bruised Skies and Unchosen Aches

I walked behind a couple laughing
The way she leaned into his side
Made me ache in places I'd forgotten
The sky above was bruised by city light
No stars tonight, only blinking ads
Selling joy in a language I don't speak
I turned corners hoping one might lead me to someone
Someone who isn't rushing home to someone else
But all I found were cold shoulders
And the ache of being surrounded
By people who've already chosen someone
And I'm still choosing no one

14. Named Voids and Forgotten Echoes

This city was supposed to be different
I came here thinking it would fill the void
But it gave it a name instead
Now I see reflections of myself
In every café window
Alone, sipping from cups too hot for comfort
Every building looms like a memory
Every alley echoes with things I forgot to say
I cross paths with thousands each day
And yet no one remembers my name
Not even the sky

15. Ghostly Steps in a Humming Dance

There's a rhythm to the city
Trains hum lullabies of movement
Lights flicker like blinking eyes watching me
I've memorized the dance
The dodging of shoulders
The nods to strangers who never nod back
I prowl through it all
Like a ghost looking for a home
Each new face just another unopened book
Too many stories, none of them mine
I want to speak, to shout, to interrupt the monotony
But I stay quiet
Because no one really listens here
Only waits for their turn to speak

16. Flickering Stillness and Skipped Pages

On the bench beneath the flickering streetlamp
I sit where I always do
Watching people move in fast-forward
Lovers brush hands
Children tug on sleeves
Friends shout greetings across the road
But I remain still
Still enough to feel the earth breathe
Still enough to wonder if I'm fading
If sitting long enough in silence
Might make me disappear altogether
No one sees me
Not really
Not even the man who asks for change
He skips me like a forgotten page

17. Teeth of the City and Silent Notes

Once I believed in connections
That people would find one another
Through books, songs, glances on trains
But this city has teeth
It chews through the soft
Spits out only what survives
I see it in the man who avoids eye contact
In the woman gripping her phone like a lifeline
In the silence between two people sitting too close
I see it in myself
The way I carry headphones without music
Just to pretend I belong
I am a lonely note in a song too fast to follow

18. Statue of Solitude and Skyward Mirrors

Even the pigeons have companions
They gather by the park fountain
Pecking at breadcrumbs, chattering in their own
language
While I sit beneath the statue
Frozen like it, forgotten like it
Every passerby sees past me
As if loneliness were invisible
As if aching had no form
I thought this place would cure me
But instead, it reflected me
A mirror held by skyscrapers
That show how small I truly am

19. Drunk Shadows and Blinking Lies

I walk late at night
When the city is drunk and raw
Streetlights throw long shadows
Taxi horns cry like tired wolves
In this hour, truth leaks out of alleys
The lovers fight louder
The lonely look longer
I stare up at the blinking signs
Hoping one will tell me what to do
Where to go
Who to be
But all it says is SALE, SALE, SALE
And I realize I've been sold an idea
Of a city that loves back
It doesn't

20. Broken Jewels and Silent Warmth

I sat beside a man crying on the steps of a closed theater
He didn't look up
And I didn't ask
Sometimes silence is the only kindness
We both stared at the wet pavement
At the way neon lights shimmered like broken jewels
Two strangers sharing a kind of nothing
But also, somehow, something
The city moved around us
But for a moment, I wasn't alone
For a breath, neither was he
Then he stood, said nothing, walked away
And I remained, holding that moment
Like a fragile cup of warmth

21. Unlit Threads in a Woven Night

The city hums like a machine I don't understand
Voices tangle in the air, a web of half-heard lives
Each window glows with someone else's story
While mine stays dark, unlit, untold
I weave through crowds, a thread pulled loose
Searching for a snag to catch me
A hand, a word, a reason to stop moving
But the streets are slick with indifference
I sit by the river's edge, where lights fracture on water
Like promises that never hold
The current whispers of escape
But I stay, pinned by the weight of being unseen
A soul adrift in a sea of motion